JUST ONCE

by Mary Blount Christian

Illustrated by Caris Lester

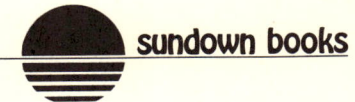

New Readers Press ● Syracuse, New York

Remembering those teachers
at Field, Hogg and Reagan
who gave me a love of words.

Edited by Wendy Stein

ISBN 0-88336-750-5

© 1982
New Readers Press
Publishing Division of Laubach Literacy International
Box 131, Syracuse, New York 13210

All rights reserved. No part of this book may be
reproduced or transmitted in any form or by any
means, electronic or mechanical, including photo-
copying, recording, or by any information storage
and retrieval system, without permission in writing
from the publisher.

Printed in the United States of America

9 8 7 6 5 4 3 2

Chapter 1

Cora pinned the diaper on her screaming baby. She picked up Sammy and patted him gently.

His screams faded into dull sobs. He buried his wet face in her shoulder.

"Be glad he cries so good now," Dr. Boyd told her. "That new milk is good for him. He's fine now."

She rubbed her cheek against Sammy's soft hair. The sweet smell of baby powder tickled her nose.

As Cora turned to leave, she felt a sharp pain in her side. She cried out.

Dr. Boyd frowned. "Are you all right, Cora? Let me check you while you're here."

"No - no!" she said sharply. More softly she added, "I've got to go. I don't have time."

The doctor let his hands fall to his sides. He sighed. "Are you sure? At least wear short sleeves, won't you? It's too hot to dress like that."

Cora nodded, looking at the floor. She was careful not to cry out again. She pushed open the door. She walked through the crowded waiting room. The people's faces were blurred through her tears.

Cora stepped from the stuffy free clinic out onto the noisy sidewalk. She held Sammy close to her and hurried east.

When Cora was a block away she finally slowed down. She sighed wearily. She could relax now. Her secret was still her own.

How could she let Dr. Boyd check her? He mustn't see. No one must see the ugly black and blue marks.

She slowly walked the two blocks to her building. She climbed the three flights of stairs. Two boys were playing with trucks in the drab hall.

Holding Sammy on one hip she pushed her key into the lock. The door to 307 swung open.

Cora chained the door shut behind her. Sammy was sleeping. Gently she put him on the bed she shared with her husband Sam.

Sammy pushed his thumb into his mouth and sucked noisily. Cora smiled. He was so beautiful. So dear.

While he slept, Cora cleaned up. Her broom brushed something shiny. It was a dime.

Cora turned it over and over in her hand. It was like a key to the outside. She could call someone on the phone with that. But who would she call?

Cora shrugged and put the dime in her dress pocket. She washed the dishes and left them to drain.

Then she looked in the cupboard. There wasn't much food there. It seemed there never was just before payday.

Spaghetti and a salad for supper tonight. Sam would like that. "When Sammy wakes, we'll go to the store," she decided. "I'll charge what I need," she told herself. "Mr. Spinoza won't mind."

Cora filled a big can with water and stepped onto the fire escape. Gently she touched the rose buds. Already a little red was peeking through. Any day now they'll burst into bloom. She was proud of her rose bushes. She grew them from cuttings. Her friend, Mrs. Farris, told her how.

Seeing those buds right here in the city gave Cora new hope. She turned to see Sammy stirring on the bed. He blinked sleepily at her, then smiled. Cora burst into a smile.

"You'll see, Sammy," Cora said. "Your daddy will be so happy. Tonight'll be different."

She shuddered. "Just once it *has* to be."

Chapter 2

Cora took Sammy with her to Spinoza's Market.

"Hello, Mr. Spinoza," she said. She put some vegetables on the counter. "Sam will pay you tomorrow."

Mr. Spinoza nodded grimly. "Cora, that's what you said last week. I can't give you much more credit. I have people to pay, too."

Cora glanced around the market. She was glad no one was there to hear him. "Please, Mr. Spinoza. Today's payday. Sam will pay you tomorrow, I promise. He just forgot last week."

Mr. Spinoza nodded. "For *you*, Cora. Not for Sam."

Cora thanked him and hurried from the store. Why did she almost have to beg? Why did she feel so guilty?

She hurried past the flower shop. But a burst of color caught her eye. She turned back and went in. She sniffed the sweet smells.

"Hi, Cora," Mrs. Farris greeted. "Hello, Sammy, little darling."

"You're just the person I wanted to see," Mrs. Farris said. "I've a big favor to ask."

"Of me?" Cora asked. "What can I do, Mrs. Farris?"

"My helper quit. I have to deliver flowers tomorrow. But I don't want to close the shop. Can you stay for an hour or two?"

Cora looked at Sammy. "But how – ?"

"Bring Sammy," Mrs. Farris said. "He can sleep in back of the counter. See? I'll fix him a little place right here. And I'll pay you four dollars an hour."

Cora grinned. "Okay, Mrs. Farris. But what if someone comes in? What if they want to buy flowers?"

"You can handle it, Cora," the woman said. "You're a smart young lady. You'll do just fine."

Cora blushed. She dipped her head shyly. "I'll be here," she said. "Thank you."

"No, thank *you!*" Mrs. Farris called as Cora left.

Cora hummed as she stirred the red sauce. Outside, the noises of the afternoon traffic grew louder.

She bathed Sammy, then fed him and put him

to bed. She spread the checkered cloth over the table. She cut a rosebud and put it in hot water to make it open quickly. She set the vase on the table.

While the spaghetti boiled, she made a salad.

The clock across the street struck six. Sam was late – again.

Chapter 3

The sun set behind the buildings across the street. The traffic thinned. Sam was late. Very late. A lump formed in her throat. Why did he *do* this? Every payday –

She heard Sam's heavy steps in the hall. There was a loud crash. Sam must have stumbled on something. Maybe one of the boys left a toy truck out there.

Cora could hear Sam mutter angrily outside the door. His key scraped against the keyhole. Cora rushed to open the door.

"What's the matter?" Sam asked, grinning at her. His face was flushed. "Are you afraid I can't find the keyhole? I haven't had that much!"

"No, Sam," Cora said. "I'm just glad you're home." She stood on tiptoes to kiss him. The odor of stale beer made her back away.

"Supper's ready," Cora said. "Why don't you wash up?"

Sam sniffed the air. "It smells *more* than ready," he said.

"Oh," Cora gasped. "It's burning!" She snatched the pot from the stove. Cora put the salad on the table. She dished the spaghetti onto the plates.

Cora tried to sound cheery. "I put on a tablecloth. And that bud's from my own bush. It looks just like Mario's Cafe, doesn't it?"

Sam grinned. "Now if you looked like Mario's waitress – "

Hot tears stung Cora's eyes. She looked away.

Sam wrapped his big arms around her. He pulled her to him. "Come on, baby. Don't you know when I'm teasing you?"

Cora tried to laugh. "I guess not, Sam. Sit down before it gets cold."

Sam pushed the spaghetti with his fork, frowning. "This stuff's like wet cement," he said.

"I'm sorry, Sam," Cora said, staring at her fork. "I thought you'd be home earlier."

"So *that's* it, huh? It's all *my* fault! Can't I stop off with a few friends?"

"Sure, Sam," Cora said hastily.

She was determined they wouldn't argue tonight. "Guess what, Sam!" she said.

"Don't be a baby. How can I guess?" Sam said angrily.

"Mrs. Farris wants me to watch her flower shop

11

tomorrow. She'll pay me four dollars an hour."

Sam's fist slammed the table. The table shook. Cora grabbed the vase before it fell.

"What's the matter? Don't you have enough work right here?" Sam raged. "Or is it the money again? You think I don't make enough money for you, don't you?"

Cora set the vase back on the table. "It's not that, Sam," she said. "It isn't like a *real* job. I just thought – "

"I *know* what you thought," Sam growled. "Spinoza met me on the walk tonight. He told me to pay my bill. Are you trying to make a fool of me?"

"No, Sam," Cora protested. "I told him you just forgot. We didn't have anything to – "

Sam stood up suddenly. The chair fell over behind him. "My wife isn't going to make me look poor and stupid! Do you hear me? I don't want you working *anywhere*, understand?"

Sam grabbed the vase. He hurled it against the wall and stomped out. The door slammed behind him.

The vase shattered. Rose petals floated in the puddle of water.

Sammy awoke crying. Cora held him close and cried with him.

Chapter 4

Cora hummed softly to Sammy. She patted his back. "Don't be scared, little darling," she whispered. "Don't be scared."

He finally relaxed and fell asleep. Cora put him back to bed. She moaned as she stood. Her side still hurt from where Sam hit her last week.

Cora knelt to pick up the broken vase. She cradled the petals in her hand. They smelled sweet – like the perfume Sam gave her once.

"He had no call to do this," she said softly. "No call at all."

After she cleaned up, she went to bed. But she couldn't sleep. She kept thinking about herself and Sam and the baby. She wished they could go back home – home to the country. But Sam was always mad there, too. Things were supposed to be better here.

She heard the key in the door. She closed her eyes and pretended to be asleep.

Sam came in, closing the door quietly. Cora didn't move. Sam went back to the door again. Then he slammed it shut.

Cora knew he wanted to wake her up. Maybe he wanted to tell her he was sorry. Or maybe he wanted to argue some more. Cora decided she wouldn't give him the chance for either.

She stayed very still, even when Sam switched on all the lights. She could see red through her eyelids. But she didn't open them.

Not this time, Sam, she thought. If I do, you might start another fight.

Sam opened and slammed drawers. He coughed and cleared his throat noisily. He seemed bound to wake her up.

Cora made herself breathe slowly in and out, just as if she were asleep.

At last Sam turned off the lights. Cora felt the bed shake as he dropped into it.

She lay still and listened. Soon his breath came slow and steady. Sam was asleep at last. She, too, drifted into a fitful sleep.

Cora woke up before Sam. She mixed some of Sammy's special milk. She put the coffee on and poured a bowl of cereal for Sam's breakfast.

Sam's eyes looked puffy and red. He stared glumly at the table. "Is that all we have?" he asked. "Just coffee and cereal?"

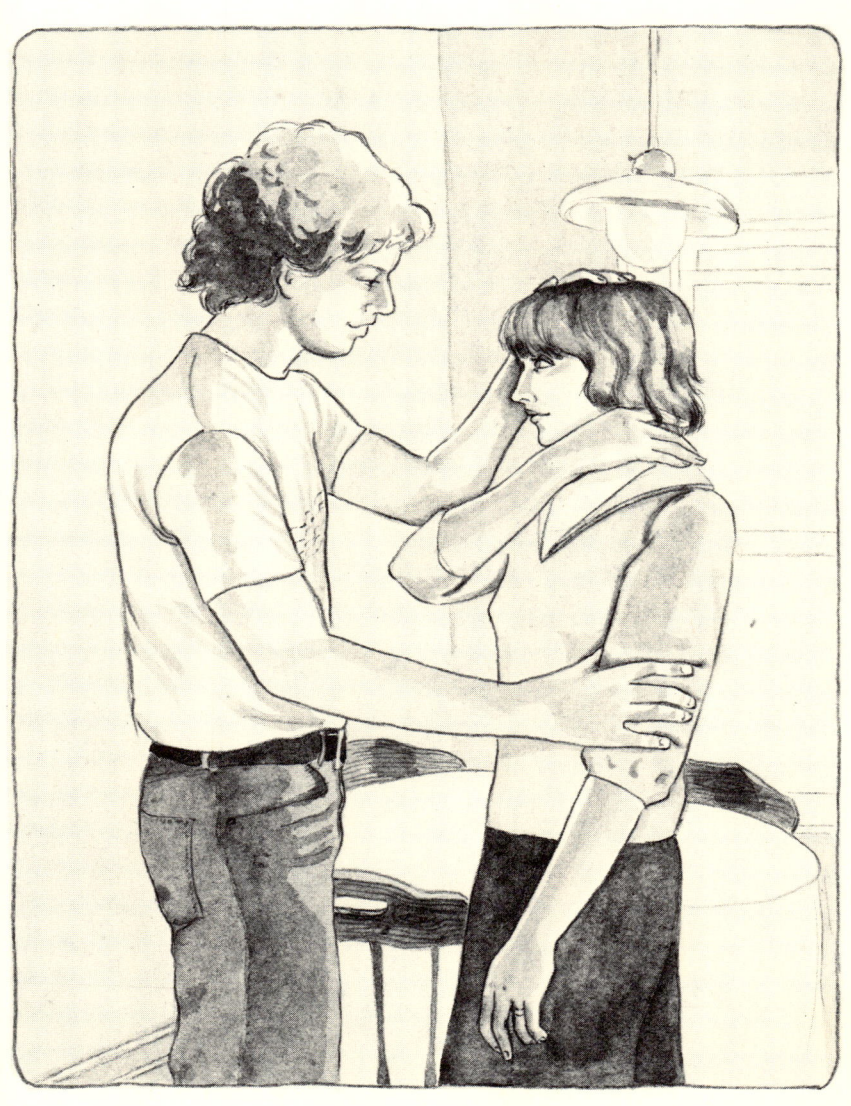

"I – " Cora stopped short with her answer. How could she answer without making Sam mad? She didn't want to say it wrong.

"I'll go to the market this morning, Sam. If that's all right with you," she added.

There, she thought to herself. Sam couldn't say she was complaining about money.

"Yeah," Sam said. "Okay. I paid Spinoza yesterday. He's got no excuse for not letting you charge now. Get something decent for a change, will you? I can't work hard when I don't eat good."

"Yes, Sam," she said.

"And maybe you should get some vitamins," he said.

"Vitamins, Sam?" Cora asked. "Do you feel bad?"

"No," Sam said. "But I think you do. You sleep so heavy – like you're too tired."

Cora turned toward the sink to hide her smile. "OK, Sam," she said.

Sam pulled Cora to him. "I love you, baby. Really, I do. I – " He hugged her and kissed her quickly. "I gotta go."

He reached to pat Sammy on the head.

"Don't forget what I said about the flower shop, Cora. You hear me?"

"I hear you, Sam," Cora said.

"You understand me now?"

"I understand."

"There's plenty to do here."

"Yes, Sam."

The door closed and Sam thumped noisily down the hall.

Cora listened until the sound was gone.

"Just once, Sam, why don't *you* understand," she sighed wearily.

Chapter 5

Cora relaxed. Sam was gone for at least eight hours. She didn't have to worry about making him mad for that long, at least.

She tried hard to forget about the flower shop. She didn't want to make Sam mad.

She stepped out on the fire escape to water her roses. Cora couldn't help but see the clock across the street. "I don't know what to do, Sammy," Cora said.

"Your daddy'll be so mad at me. It's just his pride, I guess. But I did promise Mrs. Farris. What should I do, little darling?"

Sammy gurgled.

"You're right, Sammy," Cora giggled. "I have to go. I won't take the money. That way Daddy won't get mad, will he?"

Cora hurried to the flower shop. The bell over the door rang as she pushed through.

"Cora!" Mrs. Farris said. "I was afraid you forgot."

"I didn't forget, Mrs. Farris. I – " She stopped. What could she say that Mrs. Farris would understand?

She put Sammy on the bed Mrs. Farris made behind the counter. He looked around, babbling and smiling.

"I'm not good with numbers, Mrs. Farris," Cora said. "I'm afraid I'll mess up if I have to wait on somebody."

Mrs. Farris led Cora to the cash register. "This is easy to work. Watch. Everything's priced. Read the price and then hit the same numbers here. Then hit a minus. When someone gives you their money you just hit those numbers, too. Then you hit a plus. The machine tells you how much change they get back."

Mrs. Farris showed Cora. "Pretend you sold this plant for $5.50. And say the person gave you a $10 bill."

"I'd hit five, period, five, zero, and a minus," Cora said. "Then I'd hit one, zero, period, zero, zero, and a plus."

"Right!" Mrs. Farris said. "I *told* you you were smart!"

Cora blushed. It was good to hear someone saying nice things to her.

Mrs. Farris left. Cora wiped off the vases in the window and on the shelves. She straightened the magazine rack.

The bell on the door rang. Cora could hear her

heart pounding. "Yes, sir?" she said. "Can I help you?"

"I've got some little bugs all over my roses," the man said. "I need something for them."

"I use this powder for mine," Cora said. "It works real well. Of course, you have to keep the leaves clean so they'll be healthy."

Cora tapped the numbers and held her breath. The drawer popped out and numbers flashed. She

carefully counted out the change. She put the powder in a sack.

"Come again," she called as he left.

Cora was filled with pride. She did it! And it wasn't so hard after all.

The phone rang. Someone wanted Mrs. Farris to decorate for a wedding.

Cora thumbed through the price book with pictures. "The lilies and daisies look awfully pretty," she said. "But the altar flowers and bouquets will cost you $300."

She was surprised the woman agreed. Imagine, spending that much money on flowers! She printed the woman's name and telephone number on a note pad.

Cora gave Sammy a bottle of milk. She cleaned the windows while he drank. "There now," she said. "Folks will be able to see these pretty flowers a whole lot better."

She swept, and she waited on two more people. Sammy dropped off to sleep. Cora lined up the spools on the work table. She emptied the wastebasket into the bin behind the store.

Cora couldn't think of anything else to do. So she stood at the window and watched the people go by.

Chapter 6

"Cora, you did so well!" Mrs. Farris said. "And you even sold a wedding!"

Cora could feel her face growing warm. "I'm just glad I could help you out, Mrs. Farris. It was kind of fun for me."

"Well, I just wish you'd think about working here all the time."

Cora stared at her. "Oh, no! I couldn't! Why Sam – "

"Part time, maybe?" Mrs. Farris said. "I sure could use your help. Think about it."

Mrs. Farris pushed a key on the cash register. It sprang open.

"Let's see now. I was gone two hours. That's eight dollars. And I'll round that off to ten. You should be paid for those sales, I think."

Cora backed away. "Oh, no. Please. I can't take the money, Mrs. Farris. Just think of it as a favor."

Mrs. Farris shoved the cash drawer back. "Nonsense!" she said. "I hired you. And I'm paying you. And that's that!"

"But – " Cora said.

Mrs. Farris jammed the bill into Cora's pocket. "Then I'm paying Sammy. You won't refuse money for Sammy!"

Cora glanced at Sammy. He was still sleeping. She laughed. "I guess not, Mrs. Farris. I'll take it – for Sammy."

She picked up Sammy and said good-bye.

"Think about it!" Mrs. Farris called to Cora. "I could use your help."

"Gleeee!" Sammy babbled in her ear.

Cora laughed. "You just earned $10. Is that all you can say?"

She shifted Sammy to her good side. She strolled along the street, stopping to look in store windows.

"Oh, look, Sammy!" Cora said. "Oh, what a cute outfit."

She walked inside. "Can I look at a suit like the one in the window?" she asked.

The woman led Cora to a rack. "He'd look darling in that," the saleswoman said.

"Oh!" Cora said. "I was just looking. I can't buy anything."

"It's on sale," the woman said. "It was $12.99. Now it's down to $9.00. And that includes the sales tax."

Cora's hand dropped to her pocket. She could feel the crisp bill there. "I don't – "

"He's such a cute baby," the saleswoman said. "He and that outfit are made for each other."

Cora grinned. He would look so cute. And she'd never bought him anything just for fun.

"Don't wrap it," Cora said. "I think I'll put it on him right here. I can hardly wait."

Sammy squealed and wiggled as she dressed him.

Cora frowned slightly. The suit looked cute on him. But maybe she shouldn't have bought it. He would outgrow it so soon. Still, she felt proud.

The saleswoman thought Sammy looked very handsome.

Cora carried Sammy so people could see his suit. She walked proudly down the street.

Cora smiled at strangers. Sammy gurgled. Strangers smiled back at her.

It felt so good to buy Sammy something. Not just because he needed it. Just because she wanted to.

Besides, Cora told herself, it was like getting it free. Sam didn't have to pay for it. There was no reason for him to get mad.

He'd even be proud of her, wouldn't he?

25

Chapter 7

Cora went into Mr. Spinoza's market. Mr. Spinoza thought Sammy looked great. She got the ingredients for meat loaf and carrots and applesauce. Sam loved meat loaf. And she'd make sure it didn't burn!

Mr. Spinoza handed her the charge form to sign. Cora felt a heaviness – a twinge of guilt. If she hadn't bought the suit she could have paid cash for the groceries.

No, she told herself. Sam *told* her to charge the food. But she pulled the dollar change from her pocket.

"This will pay for part of it," she said.

Mr. Spinoza changed the price. She signed and left.

Mrs. Mac, from 309, was in the hall when Cora got home. She thought Sammy looked very cute.

Cora felt so happy. Everyone thought she made a good choice. Sam would have to think so, too, wouldn't he?

She put Sammy on the floor while she mixed the meat loaf. She put it in the oven. The clock across the street showed her she had an hour.

Wouldn't Sam be surprised?

An hour passed. The meatloaf was ready. But Sam didn't come home. It wasn't payday. She wondered why he was so late? Was he hurt?

She put Sammy to bed early. She left him in his suit. Maybe he'd wake up when Sam came home. Then she could show him the suit.

She nervously ran her hands down her sides. She felt the dime in her pocket from yesterday.

It was midnight when Cora heard Sam. There was a thud. He hit the door again and again.

She jumped to let him in. He stumbled in, weaving. His face was flushed. His eyes were red. His shirt was wet and smelled of beer.

"Are – are you hungry, Sam?" Cora asked. "I'll warm the meatloaf. And – "

Sam's words were slurred. "Don't treat me like a baby. You're not my mother."

"I don't mean to, Sam. I was just worried."

"Well, you won't have to worry anymore," he said. "I'll be right here so you can keep an eye on me."

"Here, Sam?" She reached for his arm.

He jerked it away. "I've been laid off work," he said. "I don't have a job." He looked as if he might cry.

"It'll be all right, Sam," Cora said. "You'll see."

She thought of Mrs. Farris. She could work there until Sam got more work.

Sammy woke up. He whimpered fitfully.

Cora picked him up and patted him gently.

Sam rocked forward, squinting. "What's he got on? Where'd he get those clothes?"

"I – " Cora swallowed hard. "I bought them, Sam."

"You *bought* them? You mean you found some place that gave you credit? You charged clothes? Take them back. You hear?"

"I – I didn't charge them, Sam. I bought them. With my own money. Honest. I didn't spend any of your money. I even – "

Sam's eyes grew wide. He didn't wait to hear the rest. "*Your* money! You worked at the flower shop after all, didn't you? After I told you not to."

There was pounding on their wall.

"Quiet in there!" Mrs. Mac yelled. "You hush up, Sam, or we'll call the police."

Sam didn't seem to hear her or anything else. He stared at Cora. "You worked when I told you not to. *Then* you went and spent the money on something stupid."

Tears rolled down her cheeks. "It's not stupid, Sam. Mrs. Farris said I was real smart. And everybody said the outfit was – "

"You're nothing but a stupid little kid!" Sam yelled.

He drew back his fist and slammed Cora in the

face. She reeled from the sharp pain. She lost her footing and spun dizzily.

A scream echoed in her ears. She knew it was her own voice. But she couldn't stop it. She dropped to her knees and bent over Sammy. His screams blended with hers.

Cora knew there was pounding on the walls and shouts somewhere out there. But all she could think about was protecting Sammy.

The blows against her shoulders and back came again and again. She blotted them from her mind. It was as if she were somewhere else, watching.

Then she didn't feel anything at all.

Chapter 8

Cora blinked groggily. The light was painful to her. She couldn't open one eye.

She was suddenly aware. Her arms were stiff and sore. And they were empty.

"Sammy!" she screamed. "Where's Sammy?"

"Shhh," Mrs. Mac said. "He's right here, child. He's all right. Don't move. Keep that ice on your eye. It's as black as a pit. Swollen, too. And your back. Lord have mercy."

"Sam?" Cora asked. "Where's Sam?"

"He's gone, ma'am." It was a new voice.

Cora squinted toward the sound. It was a woman. She was in police uniform. Cora tried to stand, but fell back again.

"Don't try to move," the officer said. "Can you tell me what happened?"

"That ought to be obvious!" Mrs. Mac yelled. "Look at the poor child, would you?"

The officer turned back to Cora, ignoring Mrs. Mac. "Do you want to press charges? If you do we can put him in jail. Let him cool off a while."

"No – no," Cora said. "He'll cool down. He'll be sorry. He lost his job. It's his pride, you know. I act so stupid sometimes – "

"Now you hush up!" Mrs. Mac said. "You don't act stupid at all. That's a fine way for a grown man to behave – bully! He's got to learn, Cora. This isn't the first time, officer."

"You – you knew?" Cora asked. "I feel so – so ashamed!"

"You've got no call to feel ashamed," the officer said. "But you shouldn't stay here. Do you have someplace you can stay? Even if you won't press charges, you ought to get some sort of help. See the doctor, maybe?"

Cora shifted the ice pack. She winced. Her eye throbbed something awful. "I never thought about going somewhere else. This is all I got."

Mrs. Mac said, "Come over with us. I have a baseball bat if that bully tries – "

"No," Cora said. She knew Mrs. Mac meant well.

But Sam could cause trouble if he wanted to. What if he was still mad?

"If you refuse to press charges, I can't do anything more," the officer said. "But let me write down a place you can call. And we have social workers with the city, too."

She nodded and left. Cora stuck the card into her pocket. She took Sammy from Mrs. Mac.

"I'll put the chain on the door," she said. "I'm sorry to keep you awake like this."

Mrs. Mac hugged Cora. "You don't think a chain would stop that bull moose if he wants in, do you? You just yell, or hit the wall."

Mrs. Mac said good night. Cora put Sammy down on the bed.

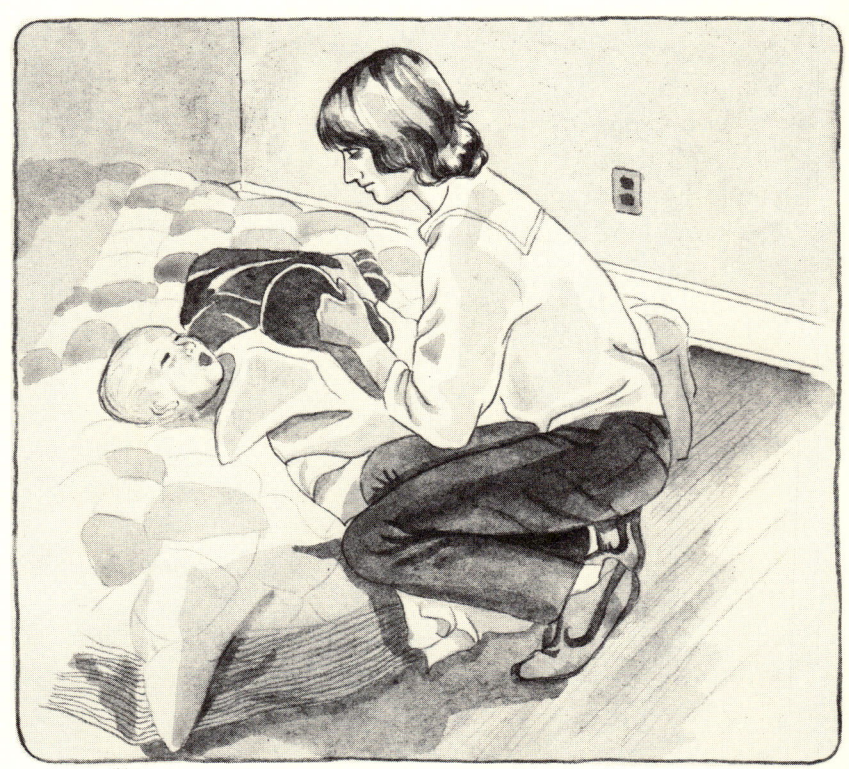

Cora sat down next to him. She just couldn't get over tonight. Sam had hit her before. Lots of times. But he'd never hit her in the face before. And this time she was holding the baby! He could've hurt Sammy.

"I can't let him hurt you, little darling," she said to the sleeping baby. "Not you."

Cora carefully rubbed her shoulder. "If I had enough to take the bus back to the country –"

She looked at Sammy in his new outfit. "Maybe it would have been a better favor if I'd bought you a bus ticket instead."

She knew the officer was right. She ought to be somewhere else. Well, she didn't have any money for a bus trip. But they could go to the bus station, anyway.

She packed Sammy's milk. She put his diapers in a sack, too. She scooped up Sammy. It was painful to walk the eight blocks. Still, she forced herself.

The bus station – a perfect place to stay awhile, Cora thought. It was full of people. It was well lit. It was open all the time.

And best of all, it was away from the apartment. It was away from Sam when he decided to come home.

Chapter 9

The station spilled light onto the dark sidewalk. Cora stepped inside. She winced as the strong light hit her swollen eye.

Cora looked around. She saw an empty seat in a long row. She eased into the seat.

She could feel the people staring at her. But she was too tired, too pained to be ashamed.

Cora looked at Sammy. He blinked sleepily. Poor little fellow, she thought. He was beginning to relax at last.

Cora set the sack of diapers and special milk on the floor by her chair. She tried to get comfortable so Sammy could sleep in her lap.

She closed her eyes against the light. A voice over the speaker announced routes. People hurried out through the back doors. Buses were waiting there.

Soon the station was quiet. There were only a few people left. Cora's head drooped. She was so tired. Maybe I could nap just a little, she thought.

Cora came awake with a start. A man was sitting next to her. He was leaning over. He was reaching for her sack.

"Stop it!" she screamed. "Stop it! Those are only diapers. That's all my baby's got!"

The man shrank from her fists as she pounded his shoulder. He jumped up and fled out the door.

Cora looked around her. People stared at her.

Weakly, she tried to explain. "He – he tried to take my baby's diapers."

The others looked away from her. They acted like they didn't want to be seen around a crazy woman.

Cora knew she didn't dare sleep again. It wasn't safe. She pushed herself to stand. It was painful.

She walked slowly around the big room. She paused to look at the posters on the wall. There were pictures of happy people everywhere. They waved and smiled. They were in front of fountains and buildings.

"See Florida," one sign said. People were playing ball and swimming. "See America," another sign said. People stood in front of the Washington Monument.

Cora sighed wearily. She saw another poster. It was by the public telephone. It was of a woman. Her face was bruised.

"You don't have to take it anymore," the sign said. "Call WIFEAID now."

Cora touched her swollen eye. Pain shot through her head. "You don't have to take it anymore," she read again.

She couldn't take her eyes off the words. With trembling hands she reached into her pocket. She pulled out the dime.

The paper the police officer gave her fell out, too. It said the same word: WIFEAID.

Cora dropped the dime in and waited for the dial tone. Then she spelled out the letters as she dialed. She didn't want to make a mistake. She had only the one dime – only the one chance.

"W-I-F-E," she said. "A-I-D." The phone rang at the other end.

Cora suddenly felt panic. She started to hang up, but she heard a woman answer.

Cora opened her mouth to speak. But suddenly the hurt and anger spilled out. She could only whimper. "I – I –"

The woman's voice was calm, soothing. "Where are you?"

Cora swallowed hard. "The bus station. East side."

"We'll be there in 20 minutes. You stay inside. We'll come in for you."

"You won't have much trouble spotting me," Cora said.

"We never do," the woman said. She sighed and hung up.

Cora stood staring at the dead phone. Had she

37

done the right thing, she wondered. She didn't even know who these people were.

The police officer knew about them. Maybe they were OK. But what about Sammy? She forgot to mention him. Maybe WIFEAID didn't want babies.

Chapter 10

Cora was still by the phone when a woman came up to her a half hour later.

She smiled at Cora and reached for the sack. "Come on. Betsy's just outside," she said.

"Betsy?" Cora said.

"Our station wagon. It's old and battered. Like some of us. But it still runs – like us."

She led Cora to a rusty, dented station wagon. Another woman inside unlocked the doors.

"I – I'm not sure why I called you," Cora said. "I – I just didn't know what to do."

"That's why the sign is there," the first woman said. "Your old man in jail?"

"Old man?" Cora asked. "Oh, you mean Sam? No. I couldn't send Sam to jail. Besides, he can't earn a living in there."

The second woman pulled into the light morning traffic. "Yeah. That's what's wrong with most

39

of us. We never learned how to dish it out – only take it."

"Velma," the first woman said. "She has to do what's best for her – and the baby. I'm Sally, by the way. This is Velma."

"Cora," she replied. "And this is Sammy. Is it all right? I mean, I can't stay any place without Sammy."

Velma laughed. "There are kids all over. Most of us have kids. That's why we stayed so long and took the battering, I guess."

The station wagon stopped in front of a dingy red brick house. The porch light was on. The front room was lit, too.

"There's no sign or anything," Cora said.

"We don't let people know. If some of the husbands knew where their wives were – "

Cora nodded. She knew only too painfully what might happen.

They climbed the front steps. "We're on call 24 hours," Velma said. "Beating up women isn't a 9-to-5 hobby."

Sally showed Cora a small room with several beds. "Get some sleep. We can talk when you feel like it," she whispered.

Cora fell asleep right away, with Sammy beside her.

When she awoke it was morning. Women and children were everywhere. Older children were getting ready for school.

Cautiously, Cora looked for something familiar. She found the living room. Velma was there.

"This is Dr. Sims," Velma said. "She's a counselor here."

The woman took Cora's hand. "I listen a lot,"she said. "And I try to help."

Cora said little all day. Mostly she watched and listened. There were 20 women and 15 children in the house.

"You don't stay here forever, hiding," Sally told Cora. "This is a halfway house."

"Halfway?" Cora asked.

"Halfway between the life you had and the one you want," Sally said.

Cora didn't comment. She didn't know what to say. She only knew that she didn't want Sam hurt. And she was tired of hurting, too.

"Some of the women go back to their men," Dr. Sims told Cora. "And some of them wind up right back here. Again and again."

"Or in the hospital – or worse," Sally said.

"Sam, you say is his name?" Velma asked. "Sam needs help to stop as much as you," she said.

"My Charlie meets me at a clinic in midtown about twice a week," Sally said. "He talks with Dr. Sims. We *both* talk to her. And sometimes we even talk to each other. Maybe one day I'll take the chance again – go back."

"No way for me and Tom," Velma said. "I'd

wind up here. But I have this job now. I can support myself soon. Then I'll move to my own apartment. Maybe I'll share one with another woman – someone like me. What about you, Cora?"

Cora shook her head and turned away. She didn't want to think about the future – not yet.

* * * *

The bruises faded and the swelling went away. And soon the other women made Cora feel at home. She talked to Dr. Sims.

"Maybe I should see Sam," she said. "Let him know that Sammy and I are all right.'"

Dr. Sims frowned. "It might be too soon for you to face him. One of us can tell him."

"Could you support yourself?" Dr. Sims asked. "If you had to, could you?"

"Mrs. Farris offered me a job at her flower shop," Cora said. "But the baby – "

"Some of the women can't work, Cora. Not yet. They can watch after Sammy right here. You can work. A few of the others do, too. You can put a little of your earnings into the grocery fund – to pay for babysitting."

"That's the only way I could stay," Cora said. "But I don't have much to wear."

Velma told Cora. "We have donated clothes. And Betsy gets everyone to work. We make out OK here."

Cora felt safe for the first time.

She called Mrs. Farris and got the job. And she talked to Dr. Sims every day.

The one thing that scared Cora was that the job was close to home. Too close, maybe, to Sam.

Chapter 11

When Cora felt healed enough, she went to work at the flower shop. She kissed Sammy good-bye and tried hard not to be scared.

Mrs. Farris was very happy with Cora's work. Cora started to heal inside as well as out.

A week after she started work, the bell on the shop door rang. Cora looked up.

"Sam!" Cora said. She held her breath waiting.

"Cora?" Sam said. "I – I heard you were here. I've come to take you home, baby."

Cora stiffened. "I'm not a baby, Sam."

He seemed startled. "I didn't mean –"

"You look thinner. Aren't you eating?"

Sam grinned at her. "Yeah. But I lost the beer fat – that's all. I haven't had any since – since that night."

Cora felt herself trembling. She struggled to control herself. She held onto the counter.

45

Sam reached out to touch her hand. She felt a rush of warmth. Cora stared at his hand over hers. The last time she saw that hand it was a fist.

It would be so easy for those powerful fingers to curl into a fist again. She tried to remember what Dr. Sims said – until Sam gets help, too, he's the same man.

"I've been watering your roses, Cora. They look real good. I washed the leaves and everything."

Cora felt a tear spill down her cheek. "Oh, Sam. Thank you. That's so sweet."

"Come home, Cora," Sam said. "Please come home. I won't hurt you anymore, I promise. I need you – you and Sammy."

Cora wanted to. She really believed all she promised in the wedding ceremony. It was supposed to be for always.

"Till death do us part." The words came to her and she shuddered. "I can't, Sam. Not for awhile. I have to *know* that things will be all right, Sam."

"They will! I promise."

"You don't know that, Sam. You *want* them to be. Just like I want them to be. But you need some help. Just like I need it."

"I'll do anything, Cora. Anything you say," Sam said.

"Anything, Sam? Then you'll talk with Dr. Sims – and me. And the other men – like you."

"Doctor? Are you talking about a *head* doctor? Cora, I don't need any head doctor. I have a job

46

again. And I stopped drinking. You and Sammy have to come home – please?"

Cora thought Sam might cry. She knew he wouldn't like to cry in front of her. She wanted to go back – to try again. But she thought about Sammy – about his nightmares.

"Dr. Sims says I don't have to come home. She says I don't have to do anything bad for me anymore. And, Sam, you're bad for me."

Sam's hand tightened over hers. Cora pulled away. "Sammy wakes up screaming in the night, Sam. What do you figure he's dreaming about? Dr. Sims says he's little, but he knows. She says he could grow up thinking hitting is *his* answer, too. I won't let that happen, Sam."

Sam's shoulders drooped in defeat. "I don't know if I can go to a head doctor – especially a woman doctor," he said. "It just isn't – manly."

Cora felt her temples throb. She remembered that night, Sam hitting her again and again. "Manly, Sam? Is beating me up manly?"

"Cora – "

Cora held up her hand to silence him. "I've got a long way to go, Sam. But I'm growing up. Maybe you can, too. That's the only way I can come home. That's a fact."

Sam scratched his chin, frowning. "I have to think about it, Cora. Where are you staying? I'll let you know."

"I can't tell you, Sam. It wouldn't be safe for the

47

women. You can tell me here what you decide."

Sam nodded and left. Cora stood at the shop window. She watched his broad back as he walked toward home. Somehow he didn't look so scary anymore.

More than anything, Cora wanted them to be a family again. She wanted to run after Sam, to tell him. But she didn't. With the help of Dr. Sims and the others, she'd wait.

It could be a long time – or never. But Cora knew she'd be all right – she and Sammy.

"I'm not dumb," she thought. "I can learn to take care of money. To cook better. To make a good home for us."

With or without Sam, they'd be OK, she promised herself. If she went back to Sam, it had to be *her* choice. Not because she had to, but because she *wanted* to.

The bell over the door jangled. Cora stepped forward and smiled.

"May I help you, ma'am?"